T0344632

THE HUGH MacLENNAN POETRY SERIES

Editors: Allan Hepburn and Carolyn Smart

whereabouts

EDWARD CARSON

McGill-Queen's University Press

Montreal & Kingston • London • Chicago

ISBN 978-0-2280-0632-9 (paper)
ISBN 978-0-2280-0716-6 (ePDF)
ISBN 978-0-2280-0717-3 (ePUB)

Legal deposit third quarter 2021
Bibliothèque nationale du Québec

Printed in Canada on acid-free paper that is 100% ancient forest free
(100% post-consumer recycled), processed chlorine free

Financé par le gouvernement du Canada   Funded by the Government of Canada | Conseil des arts du Canada   Canada Council for the Arts

We acknowledge the support of the Canada Council for the Arts.

Nous remercions le Conseil des arts du Canada de son soutien.

Library and Archives Canada Cataloguing in Publication

Title: whereabouts/Edward Carson.

Names: Carson, Edward, 1948– author.

Series: Hugh MacLennan poetry series.

Description: Series statement: The Hugh MacLennan poetry series

Identifiers: Canadiana (print) 20210172991 | Canadiana (ebook)
20210173025 | ISBN 9780228006329 (softcover) |
ISBN 9780228007166 (PDF) | ISBN 9780228007173 (ePUB)
Subjects: LCGFT: Poetry.

Classification: LCC PS8555.A7724 W44 2021 | DDC C811/.54—dc23

This book was typeset by Marquis Interscript in 9.5/13 Sabon.

for Lillian and Roy
wherever you are

CONTENTS

WHEREABOUTS

One not lost finds no way
A.R. Ammons

THEREABOUTS

(OR THE MAPMAKER'S DILEMMA)

It is not down in any map; true places never are
Herman Melville

IN THE POEM

of the world
there once

was a map
of the map

composed in
the likeness

of a poem
where the

poem is a
map of the

ready mind
escaping

everywhere
into words

in darkness
or daylight

intimacies
of thought

are common
destinations

embracing
different

directions
or common

directions
promoting

different
destinations

DISTORTION

in a map
is a wily

distraction
to the eye

a dilemma
of disruption

in a mind
asking if

scope in a
world this

size and
breadth is

nearby or
far fetched

CONTIGUOUS

latitudes
of belief

breezily
plumb

longitudinal
dialogues

inhaling
exhaling

swirling
discourses

triggering
tremblings

in faraway
willows

A MAP IS

the smell
of far flung

the savour
of here to

there tasting
metaphorical

a menu of
possibilities

navigating
panoptic

designated
panoramas

starved of
their shape

COLONIZING A

continent in
space time

divulges its
orientation

determines
its purpose

and arrogates
delimitation

stitching in
confinement

its power
a dubious

image of
the world

THE BRAIN IS

a lone self
organizing

covert map
a rhizomatic

arabesque of
propulsive

nodes roots
shoots buds

the esemplastic
mind sensing

this is but
another form

of amorphous
transformation

MERCURIAL

this brain
its aporia

unfolding
the map

of its being .
into another

image from
rhumb lines

to meridians
all neurons

triangulating
passageways

solving what
to think next

THOUGHTS OF A

stream run
into slower

lakes spawn
wider rivers

rapids then
tumble on to

a confluence
where a man

and a woman
meet to say

where they
have come

from maybe
also going to

FLIRTATIONS

with fields
bristle all

thoughts of
verisimilitude

the twitch
of survey

and slick
of terrain

flourish at
peripheries

the swidden
burns swells

heightening
with lure

THERMODYNAMIC

aberrations
in adjacent

locations or
refractions

of thought
will cook

up neuronal
calculations

phase in
transitions

map a mind
as the poem

confronting a
critical degree

the rapidly
blossoming

scans of
the brain

liberate a
portrait of

arousal or
the merely

biological
a state of

mind and
interpretation

thought to
be equivocal

WOOZY IN LOVE

the *musica
humana*

is a back to
back systole

and diastole
the harmonics

of the brain
keeping time

with giddy
interludes

of scrumbled
proximities

devising new
places to be

AT THE END

of the road
where the

poem ends
the fireflies

haphazardly
persuasive

anticipate a
conversation

pretend to
be neurons

of what we
think is the

thought but
seldom is

HEREABOUTS

Tomorrow is easy, but today is uncharted
John Ashbery

Each one of the 86 billion neurons found in the average
adult brain can establish links to and share signals
with up to 10,000 other neurons by means
of as many as 500 trillion available
synaptic connections.

The MNI (Montreal Neurological Institute and Hospital)
coordinate system and atlas for the human brain is
a neuroscience brain mapping template used as
a statistical parametric mapping technique
for neuroimaging brain activity linked to specific
mental processes.

the tug pull push pluck press of a neuron
as it throttles ahead of thoughts around it

become in the mind a difference of scale
the patterns of beauty and calculation of

a likeness being one and the same or an
equivalence of resemblance tied to a map

of parametric coordinates in the brain for
any X figure sitting at the intersection of

Y for the family Z of neurons analogous
to a painting of sunflowers in an earthen

pot in a large yellow house found in Arles
the flowers themselves a meditation on the

fluctuations of time the forms and lines of
the petals and stems an atlas of emotions

MNI axis x = -36 y = 33 z = 24

proposing a map like no other in the
size of a mind the mind is a weather

of its own making where any proximity
to you is both nearby and far not unlike

a fever within a body provoking a hot
and cold feeling where we can't be this

close together or too long apart never
realizing how it just might be possible

our love is the lightning then thunder
a frenzy of seeing then hearing that

speaks clear and true to this intimacy
counting 1 2 3 4 ... seconds marking

miles to locations in outlying settings
anywhere between everywhere and here

MNI $axis\ x = -12\ \ y = -55\ \ z = 66$

at times composed or more often than
not buoyant our relationship travels from

A to B in morphologies of pleasure and
release at times an embrace of external

lure and resistance the way water at rest
naturally supports the light as air insect

skating across its surface or perhaps like
this pooling of words and balancing of

clearcut motives scenarios and surfaces
but where conditions warrant the mind

meanders toward love's peripheries the
outskirts of a radius where feeling is a

deeper discourse calmer in its heart of
intention more agitated in its impatience

MNI *axis* $x = -30$ $y = -66$ $z = 42$

the quiver stretch shudder of matter and
energy the slow accretion of cells adding

up to an image of you mapped into the
cortex is in fact a brief composite array

of excited neurons a choreography and
a somersaulting into being so that the

question of your likeness its image and
outline eagerly materializing into plain

view for all to see will come into focus
virtually the second a thought of you is

unleashed along a brain's cagey corridors
the pitch switch and tumble of shuttling

intensities revealing the little known and
unknowable near misses consuming sight

MNI axis $x = -18$ $y = -42$ $z = -6$

VENTROINTERMEDIAL THALAMUS

where a river thinks of its waters even
interrupts its calm or hampers its flow

willing it to crumble teeter topple carve
the curve of its shore what emerges is a

current beneath the surface of a thought
meaning what we think of as things are

without doubt the give and take between a
thing and its thought but can never be the

thought or thing itself so we begin to see
how in the river of its need a mind will

respond to the slow ebb or faster flow the
random engagement and hit and miss mass

of thought irreconcilable in substance harder
still to untangle account for as real enough

MNI axis $x = 9$ $y = -6$ $z = 18$

LEFT POSTERIOR PARIETAL LOBE

where language and thought are ciphers
the likeness of you in countless images

crops up only after you begin to appear
unmoored from the very thought of you

descending stairs your body steps ahead
a figure in time-lapse motion captured

cautiously aroused impatiently seductive
the brain a geography of amorous need

as well as dissonance where the simple
look of you is a portrait of meticulous

neuronal signals prompts and triggers
evolving points of view both accurate

and contrary both coupled and detached
a provocation of abstraction into shape

MNI $axis\ x = 7\ \ y = 9\ \ z = -52$

perhaps we are lovers but certainly we
are birds emerging out of the back of

the mind arrayed in long lines of flight
where every human uncertainty turns up

as puzzling silhouettes cautiously hoping
to turn comparison into something more

than an expression of near and far or the
distance between us being closer here and

everywhere farther and larger than a map
of our need where a brain never at rest

relentlessly roams in biologic breezes of
consciousness simmering in thoughts that

emerge from locations calculated to find us
enduring in belonging restive in becoming

MNI axis x = -54 y = 2 z = -8

a voice newly arriving out of nowhere
materializing in the heart of night like

Plato calling from domains elegant and
wise is the mind baffled by its terrain

of sounds with each word pulsing yet
it's you who metamorphoses everything

your eyes anxiously glancing behind to
a space difficult to define between us a

mix of precision and ambiguity escapes
towards a new anamnesis deftly entering

the field hoping to think like a feeling
and feel like a propagation of the past

set to step away from the background
a foreground streaming into the frame

MNI *axis x = -20 y = -30 z = -8*

the throb of an artery navigates all angles
in the brain continues here and there then

quickens to flow though never subject to
the same dispersion it finds places of rest

and slows pours forward sometimes with
a reckless abandon into the blue cataracts

and hasty white pools of the mind where
yearning is a dilemma of intention always

rising or dipping distracting itself through
tributaries with destinations near enough

to think about but too far away to know
the outlying spaces between us as distant

as ever these waters carrying us along in
a flawless portrait of a mind looking out

MNI axis x = -12 y = -18 z = 18

inside an otherwise infinite mind there is
a nuanced zig or zag of a wind breezing

by on continuous neuron circuits in which
synaptic parts input crisscross and output

bring into being in a suitably elastic way
world-making thoughts in shapes reaching

out to asymmetrical assortments of novel
words opening up outward into unlimited

adaptations of puff or squall gust or gale
a breathing in out in out where a flutter

of repercussions delivers agile expressions
multiplying contracting arousing appeasing

this wind the never-ending notion of self
this mind the perfect accident of absolute

MNI axis x = -45 y = -60 z = 30

when the mind needs to be free of itself
to be where it wishes to go it will gain

ground little by little imperceptibly self-
possessed craving to travel the map of

its being and compass of its coming or
going until it reaches a time and place

far away as needed from where it was
and there in those outlying explorations

a singular pleasure of arousal populates
a common and collective understanding

a place of escalating appetite receptive
to forces of desire both impulsive and

willfully chasing lines of exit or entry
intimacy always a difference close by

MNI axis $x = 39$ $y = -58$ $z = 50$

not always evident in tide or current we
couple uncouple from one another always

half spent or halfway to go desire is far
more peripatetic than one might expect a

fast forwarding to an emotional return in
itself an often overwrought anticipation we

learn time and time again to love to lean
headlong into it then draw back with the

best intentions our words soaking into the
ether between us where language embraces

both absence as well as itinerant obsession
an eloquence of temptation and trust found

to be everything it professes to be freeing
the simplest idea as well as most arousing

MNI *axis* $x = 8$ $y = 28$ $z = -22$

thought will go where it needs to much
as a river naturally follows or overflows

its banks a hazard likely to trigger fear
or risk of a worry a response to pressure

or possibly a blend of tension and fright
as a feeling of alarm emerging in a mind

quickly doubles back upon itself over and
over again continually fretfully conversing

with the hippocampus overtaking certainly
overwhelming feelings in electrochemical

flooding of the deeply wired passageways
in the brain where reason is everywhere

wanting sense wanting feel wanting flee
a language of emotion pouring itself free

MNI axis x = 28 y = 4 z = -18

MEDIAL PREFRONTAL CORTEX

don't take my heart don't break my heart
acting as if there is no longer ever after

the time arrives when after ever becomes
a sharper notion of mind in front of the

heart of a thought the sense of what has
come and gone no longer adding up to

any meaning of love or love of meaning
but a lucid thing nevertheless a stillness

held between tranquility and commotion
the heart at odds with itself as too little

comes from so much before yet a mind
resists holds back in the hush persists

in its pathway of recognition recognizing
a grave heart trembles not knowing itself

MNI axis x = -51 y = -69 z = 21

WHEREABOUTS

(THE LOVERS' DISCOURSE)

we need a science, or perhaps an art, of distances
Roland Barthes

contrary to what you may think there's more

to a rat a tat tat of time she says yet only in

aftertime will truth be told of any questions

or those not or seldom asked so hereafter he

says be mindful that at the stroke of now a

passionate mind won't know a why or when

of where she says which is an arrow and also

tyrant of time where brief degrees or minutes

are measures appearing out of nowhere being

neither middle nor margins of a beginning or

end to speak of and what the mind reveals in

a before and after organizing of love's timely

way of locating what's here and now is in a

nick of time arriving not a moment too soon

FORCE THAT MAKES UP IN TIME
WHAT IT LOSES IN SPEED

our poem largely speeds or strolls she

says our conversations pressing smooth

the ups or downs withholding time to

facilitate an exit or an entry a pause

or continuity he says such a sonnet is

comma-free in thoughts permeating like

groundwater percolating memories and

arguments she says our love has time

enough to set words straight whether

fast or slow it's not enough to shake

out more head less heart more heart

less head but better to know where

there is either a beginning or an end

a current's pull is what we recommend

poem is space and serpentine and he says

she says it worries in human neural time

but it is always a river weighing what the

mind wants to think about she says to go

where it needs to go its waters in a pull

pour of close embrace its desire all linger

want and way in the way a feeling in a

probing mind is what might come to pass

he says while setting in motion this brief

chat there's the time a poem takes to tour

the hidden orbits of drift surge tumble or

rise in the tangle chatter swarm and knot

of a brain in which all outcomes are near

misses unbearably close randomly remote

ALL BY MYSELF DON'T WANT TO BE
ALL BY MYSELF

meeting for the first time that scent of her

suffuses the air a certain snare of certainty

worn in pulse points at the ear neck wrist

he says what's that you're wearing and she

says slyly leaning into the conversation my

perfume or blouse maybe both he says not

ready yet to play but willing to puzzle out

how best to make sense of making sense

she says not everything has to be a riddle

to be solved perhaps in this the unwritten

rule is in holding something back he says

a woman will always have more questions

than a man has answers while a man says

what he should have said only when alone

best first to find then seek she says and

listen next then speak the words of what

will follow the way eager twilight curves

night's starry sweep he says we all wish

for signs of what can loop together things

or pull them apart so when a man thinks

like a woman and a woman thinks like a

man an inflection in their words diverges

luring each from one direction to another

so speak with me she says and say you

feel this shimmering pressure binding us

iridescent in its fearful intimacy he says

this perfume of tension this scent of his

and hers will love in conflict or caress

lust he says is a shadow filling the room

though quite unlike the actuality she says

a desire without empathy is less metaphor

than mind fitfully advancing or retreating

a cimmerian brume of hesitation and need

where the coarse kiss of appetite becomes

a concern at the very last second and the

unforeseen occurs she says in a prickle of

caution the door whooshing open as *words*

fly out of our mouths like threatened birds

startled in the unmoored know how of no

and consent the distance between what is

welcomed or not the displeasure of denial

in the mind flexing rising up fiercely dark

you were always on my mind he says an

observation not so entirely convincing she

suspects not near to what he means yet

a presence accurate enough to implant an

image in the rising sun of her recollection

she says the way light stretches the room

saturates the path it negotiates at the only

speed it will ever know but in the event

of time away he says maybe a rose might

do as a reminder not all is what it seems

to be as inconsistent as that might sound

a warm blooded physics of deep memory

the often unseen impact between a belief

and the intangible sense of what to think

beautiful or not there is a man she says a

man never too close and always too far a

man of sparkle and spit bluster and lure

he says beyond all pleasure past and all

to come such beauty is in the eye of the

beholder yet difficult to know what makes

him as he is she says unwavering in one

way not so in another but given the time

all living things will find an end and so

if love is sometimes blind then a man is

clearly an unclear image of ambiguity or

dodge of authenticity where on the outside

looking in the essence of appearance is a

choreography seldom seen rarely realized

listen to this and pay attention to how it's

said she says be ready also to ask uneasy

questions and try try not to be distracted

by mental side trips or diverging notions

and the like so we might meet up later

where life goes on goes on goes where

if one can journey back towards another

he says all love is momentary within a

life then vanishes or if with hardly time

to spare it dawdles in mid-mind to find

arrays of versatile exploration she says

let me lead you into these poems where

at every turn thinking this can't be you

we hear anxious pleasure speaking out

EMBODIED SUBJECT
AND FRAGMENTED OBJECT

when something *seems* rather than *is* or

when *nothing* turns out to be *something*

questions arise she says in a tête à tête

that is inching us cautiously forward or

drawing us back each time spilling over

against obstacles he says the way a mind

resists and the words respond finding any

way around articulate variations of puzzles

to a quotient of closeness or confusion she

says it makes me hungry and tired getting

to know all about you it's an all day and

all night job where you listen then stray

a relationship one part Picasso riven into

pieces the other implausibly reassembled

a plumey and quizzical harmony is in

the air she says a fiery rhythm raising

a rambunctious then crackling mischief

he says pitching headlong into her flesh

a kiss then pausing pulls away returns

unexpected to breasts cupped contrary

fingers looping nipples falling to hands

and knees hips cresting thighs shivery

running slick and parting but never in

mind she says always somewhere else

pushing pushing back miles away this

body switching over itself where it is

breathing in letting go breathe and go

a mind apart together a song a static

LOVE IS A DIFFICULT CAUSE
TO DEMONSTRATE

buried deep inside she says you fill things

up with that feeling of being occupied by

something hard to resist he says stretching

open pushing the walls aside is a balance

we keep a pressure of squeeze and release

as together we rock forward and back she

says if a man is involved his cock is sure

to follow never far away for this must be

his happiness he says as well as confusion

that muscles itself between mind body and

the outside world she says a man dwells

within one life whereas a woman lives in

several more but seldom one of her own

a feeling more remote than close-at-hand

when you're not here she says anxious

to give comfort and explain an absence

or you're not where you're meant to be

this *here* might not be where you think

it is so possibly absence is a deception

some of the time exceedingly difficult

to pinpoint trickier still to transition to

the space a body steps into withdrawing

its image slowly ever so slightly rarely

seen as turning away from another or

disavowal of the body rather what the

mind makes of a presence gone without

going where every distance is mysterious

a space-time reshuffling all moving parts

the perils of *this is that* will soon turn

to linear lateral endless deliberations of

a concept he says both rational and also

unreasonable while she says a preference

for what is literal suits best but he says

no something more along the lines of a

predilection for the abstract neither one

of which would seem either an absolute

or relative truth and yet when a thought

builds sequentially as in one upon another

or each word is subject and subconscious

content the conclusion is a culmination

of the mind reproducing itself in a poem

this ever present death defying possibility

PETITE SONATINE CANTIQUE

argue argue argue with me endlessly she

says in a squabble bicker scrap and spat

her anger muscling the words from first

to last a promise of leaving no thought

unsaid not even a quibble or grumble

unbending this or that and so it goes

when all is said and done in minutes

to seconds he says this knowing knows

whatever is thought is where one has

to go and yet this argument might be

leaning into words of harsh extremities

blinkered often routinely unconditional in

returning to a hurly burly of the moment

in which persuasion is a dubious success

RHETORICAL PAWNS IN UNWINNABLE ARGUMENTS

feeling mostly reasonable he says you're

becoming hysterical predictably irrational

she says you confuse the power to argue

with the emotional behaviour of a uterus

while such exchanges are not whirlwinds

of reaction but the quick fire commotion

elasticity and commerce of give and take

he says no amount of rhetoric can rescue

this spat either as a saving of time while

adding to it or both pruning and growing

the power that feeds it she says it's just

the law of physics that seeks out inverse

states of energy more like gravity pressing

up not down or critical quiet at its loudest

a swift answer he says is better than a

slow silence while she says better to be

swift to hear than slow to speak a fine

delicacy no doubt for those well versed

in questions and the stories they expose

of unresolved emotions anxiety or love

while any hesitation he says is a mind

confusing what it thinks for what is true

then plainly speaks in a voice reaching

out holding forth but in a field of rogue

communication she says a man says yes

without a thought whereas a woman is

more persuaded to say tell me how this

ends or will it mean the same tomorrow

AFTER AN ARGUMENT THE DARK MIND
OF NIGHT

being up front about how a man thinks

she says is an ongoing tussle of fidelity

while he says any argument of this sort

speaks to incidents recalled or self asides

a kind of hindsight where there's pleasure

then penance possibly retribution the kind

she says where laughing comes to crying

a meeting of bodies rubbing up against a

way of thinking that rises falls then finds

a passion of feeling or failing and guilt

he says in much of this the *error is too*

early regret is too late being neither a

figure of opposition nor comfort of hope

her final words a constellation of sorrow

in the absence of evidence to the contrary

a woman plays to compliance in order to

win control she says like a canny gambit

or come as you are affection trading open

intimacy rich in strategy and subtlety for

explanations of things as they are he says

the art of dominance or autonomy is not

issues of yes or no say or suppress but is

found deep in a perpetual motion the give

and take the dip reel whorl of convenience

or resolve she says love is never enough

or without cost as too often a man thinks

free will says or does what serves at the

time while a woman simply knows better

there's no schematic for what happens

only what she says laid out in a map

both coterminous and hypothetical and

yet it is not about a thought but what

is *re*thought in the saying much like

the seasons he says following filtering

one another then all over again in the

writing a composite weather of change

offering a sense of now a candor once

removed from revision edited cut back

then added to the whole its appearance

of presence laying claim to the current

each thought nosing surfacing its way

from mind into being impossibly here

in lopsided layers of reason she says and

with words twittering in fidgets of fluster

there is vigilance and selection distraction

distance and alignment all pertinent to a

rhetoric of the male need to quarrel over

what if or *suppose* he says each is crucial

should thought stumble or come apart yet

where conditions allow a plain typology

of profile order and taxonomy is a proof

of where language swerves south into a

history of red herrings smoke screens or

camouflage an appreciation for which she

says whispering such is a secret revealing

and concealing us within that imminence

be still she says to no one in particular

yet aspen leaves will flutter and dance

in the barest of breeze be still he says

bellowing across in a clamorous voice

words she says in a pensive mood *are*

crude and they're also too busy to be

mistaken for the faintest wind or soft

tremblings of trees each impossibly real

in a meadow teeming in autumn flame

yet aspen leaves will flutter and dance

falling away with a capricious twitch

she says where nothing remains as it

is and every word containing us abides

all distance brimming evolving this vast

evening sunlight faltering is a melancholy

of sorts she says its radiant meme of love

adrift the most deceptive of sorrows where

feeling is both repressed and welcomed he

says paradoxically more fading expectation

or misplaced lingering desire tied to what

can only be approached but never reached

she says impatient in the twilight air to

prolong this singularity our love is rarely

what it's meant to be unknown as we are

to ourselves in times when *self deception*

remains the most difficult deception where

that physical shudder of resistance is the

counterbalance to the mind lying to itself

difficult woman indifferent man having

quarrels she says in replays of choices

showing up as what ifs or hypothetical

arrays each an iteration in real time in

search of a way out he says it appears

all this is personal and she says some

problems are obstacles to leap over her

laugh a burst of delight in a frisson of

sound and denial that deliciously evades

his grasp he says every word speaks of

pleasure and pain like a polished stone

skipping across a pond at once repetitive

until its end but always worth repeating

until one's voice is scarcely recognizable

most men are afraid to be vulnerable she

says a minute or more into it will render

them sullenly off kilter all their thoughts

cartwheeling into each other he says it's

a confusion of self-control and swagger

not a reliable way out of the usual way

of pulling yourself together she says it's

a delicate equation that both relinquishes

strength as well as enlarges it while still

uncertain what to hand over or hold back

he says this has never happened before

well none of it changes a thing she says

the more felt the less exposed condensed

abbreviated is a different burden of love

A MAN LIKE A WOMAN LIKE A MAN

in you from behind she says adjusting her

strap-on a tattoo in the arch of his back

twitching with each stroke he says this is

no cockfight or crisis of design but more

a reversal and collaboration front to back

her to him she says what some might call

wanton yet others see a blithe *sprezzatura*

like an embrace of animus and anima or

mask of disguise and true desire he says

one of us is lying our double talk an art

of reticence and nonchalance cagey in its

lack of modesty beguiling in its control

she says we meet here in the middlemost

of two coaxing together this fierce need

in their heart men and women admit this

need she says to nurture a fantasy to be

with someone else if only for the time it

takes for common sense to arrive killing

off the crush and giddy blush of attention

he says that need to feel wanted can go

a long way to guilt and angst in which a

flirty come on and turn on is a siren song

that appears only when we least expect it

though it's really a thought about feeling

that something is missing an empty look

or desire in doubt that hesitates and then

soon enough evaporates the soft geography

of the mind hunting for another to embrace

science says the better half really is better

she says what moves through the mind of

a man is the default male one size fits me

approach with only one X to speak of he

says X marks the spot where an extra X

makes a woman while a Y will make all

the difference she says and any distinction

of best is an opportunity to address older

mutable differences while he says gender

might be unsteady some of the time but

so is a bicycle the mind will muscle its

way through the real slope and splay of

hormones all our parts always this close

or this far apart from what is truly us

the brief static of our discourse she says

is neither unchanging nor motionless nor

is it the hiss fizz crackle pop of an airy

interference looking for somewhere to go

with no way to get there he says who's

going anywhere anyway and why is this

mostly a dilemma of knowing more than

thinking more then asking where an idea

begins or ends or what could it be made

of she says difficult as that might sound

or feel but it's precisely this feeling he

says that is also a weaving of sorts like

a haphazard thermal imbalance suddenly

the fleeting molecular physics of words

THE EMPTY GLANCE OF A KNOWING
OBSERVER

in men she says a woman as body mindset

is sex waiting to happen even though it is

nothing like the actual thing where desire

takes the shape that it takes he says not

all men surely hopefully as pleasure with

no compassion is giving with one hand

while taking with the other and she says

no not every man but there's no way of

knowing when desire appears in a guise

unexpected a pairing of flesh unintended

like magnets both attracting and if turned

around an aversion sidestepping skimming

away keeping intimacy at length the rush

of a continuous emptiness body to body

a clit she says is a peculiar wisp cloaking

then coming out of itself replying mightily

to touch or something he says to embrocate

to tamper with or to tenderly moisten with

a kiss she says when taken whole its nerves

unmoor as sense travels top to bottom back

to front becoming that first part of a puzzle

where a curve or straight line matters most

he says it's all irony of geometry or shape

where nature knows too much of a good

thing soon becomes what is never enough

laying bare the mathematics of a stimulus

that when things come to a head it's over

in a jiffy multiplication a likely addition

knowing already where this will end up

she says what was asked of you is what

was said so to repeat follow me on this

lick me here no not there here just fine

a guide suitably enthusiastic enough for

two he says a tease and please face-first

slide with tongue and nose headlong to

plunge and penetrate patience she says

slower arrives stronger expectation needs

dedication a teetering tongue close by is

the calculus more or less of suck press

circle squeeze the rub slide kiss he says

of communication like asking one thing

hearing another mixed feelings all over

LISTEN LISTEN LISTEN

you listen to my voice she says and yet

you hear it in that way a man hears

an empty room the way a man at a loss

for words conspires with that loss where

hearing has a way of modifying what a

voice has said he says or what a mind

of words resisting words thinks it hears

is in fact a narrative basking in telling

the story of our own wanting a man she

says who is listening to an empty room

where a spring moon flooding down from

above casts a shadow of a voice making

known what is missed being missed not

a darkness to be left unnoticed unfilled

IN THE WAY THAT MOST
OF THE WIND HAPPENS

in the size of a world she says a man

with no one to speak to but himself is

the loneliest man a man most remote in

his mind he says his thought is a wind

in the shape of a word where there is

no centre but only himself so the wind

wheels and rambles she says it speaks

a melodic sound of tintinnabulation in

a world where a tree will not bend nor

its branches swirl with the birds singing

there he says that a voice needs another

alone will not do it's more than merely

overwhelming breathtaking heartbreaking

a wind is motion longing to be moved

too often a brief touch away from himself

never near enough to a real feel of things

he says her skirt is a silky consciousness

of risk and lure holding her closer in an

intimate wrap she says the way each tuck

or fold will map her every move and yet

this is not for the pleasure of a man but

instead a paradox like an undertow pulling

against the tide wanting everywhere to be

seen and nowhere talked about and equally

seen nowhere but everywhere talked about

these are he says dense eddies of troubling

conversation where the mind has a way of

transposing what a body feels it perceives

beguiling accomplished tempting at times

an object of consumption that is always

fuckable she says a woman's lot is too

often a lost pound or face cream away

from attraction he says it's all about an

ambiance a feeling a mood becoming a

stereotype paired to an emotional contour

easy for you to say she says but when it

comes to love it often ends in a binary

of mind and body of thought and feeling

a *you'll go your way I'll go mine* or a

damned if you do damned if you don't

calculation of unforgiving love composed

in the unapproachable shape of the mind

held tight in the mind when your tongue

disappears beneath me she says it is not

a coarse invitation or anticipation of sex

but a stillness where a release of desire

is the strength of such silence he says

need steals away the breath as it filters

down the spine filling loins with blood

buzz and tremble she says such arousal

is an absence growing into itself whether

offered or received it's the slower dense

trickle of desire yet for many it is easy

as a breeze or breath taken in what a

flightless bird knows in its heart awaits

after the limb after the muscles let go

want and *need* aren't the same she says

though hand in hand they share a place

of surrender looking for a common sense

of shared emotion while he says maybe

there's ground between desire and craving

where a longing splits two ways teaching

the difference is to yield in body but not

in spirit she says it's where a man feels

no more than what he wishes to believe

whereas what a woman believes she feels

with all her heart he says *want* makes us

think too much unmasks both weaknesses

and strength while *need* has the hot smell

of absence a fever finding no real thought

there's porousness at the borders of our

love she says where disbelief skepticism

inkling hover wanting to be free wanting

to belong to wade past misunderstandings

misconceptions he says if it's love you're

worried about then give it away the way

when a man and woman talk there's love

of common sense or a shared disavowal

each differently understood a dark matter

she says of the person within the words

where thought is a form of resistance to

communication or where resistance he says

in the form of a thought is a suppression

of promising parts made willful consuming

a knowing eloquence is heard but poetry

is overheard in the flurry of our dialogue

we press compress ourselves our contours

on a page propagating a mind's fine print

of both disclosure and reticence she says

one must be a lover to be in a poem

when no one knows where it's going to

where no one knows what happens next

he says everything must go somewhere

though even in motion there must be a

suspension to wait for that summons to

another place she says so in every mind

there is a voice at hand that holds it also

modifies all that is thought in its saying

NOTES AND ACKNOWLEDGMENTS

As always, I am deeply grateful to the wise eyes of Brian Henderson and Allan Hepburn; both discerning and creative, precise and generous, the one unerringly spies what I'd hoped to say while the other never misses what I'd failed to see.

"One not lost finds no way," A.R. Ammons, "The Way of One's Desire," *The Complete Poems of A.R. Ammons: Volume 2.* W.W. Norton & Company, 2017. 364.

"It is not down in any map; true places never are," Herman Melville, "Chapter 12: Biographical," *Moby-Dick or The Whale.* 150th anniversary issue. Penguin Books, 2001. 61.

"Tomorrow is easy, but today is uncharted," John Ashbery, "Self-Portrait in a Convex Mirror," *Self-Portrait in a Convex Mirror.* Penguin Books, 1972. 71.

The poems "right lingual gyrus occipital lobe" and "left angular gyrus parietal lobe" first appeared in slightly altered forms in the *Malahat Review* 210, Spring 2020. 84-6.

In "medial prefrontal cortex" the quote "don't take my heart don't break my heart" is from "Head Over Heels," by Tears for Fears, 1990, with lyrics by Curt Smith and Roland Orzabal, on *Songs from the Big Chair.*

"We need a science, or perhaps an art, of distances,"
Roland Barthes, *How to Live Together: Novelistic
Simulations of Some Everyday Spaces*. Translated by Kate
Briggs. Columbia University Press, 2012. (Originally given
as a lecture, College de France, 1977.)

"Amare chronos kairos aevum," in the prologue of
"whereabouts," is a scrumbling of Italian, Greek, and Latin
words from Wikipedia combining "to love" (amare) with
three different ways of experiencing time: chronological
or sequential (chronos), which is quantitative time; the
right or opportune moment for action (kairos), which is
qualitative time; and the "improper eternity" (aevum),
which is the mode of existence experienced by angels, a
state between the timelessness of God and the temporal
experience of material beings.

The title "force that makes up in time what it loses in
speed," is from John Ashbery, "The Short Answer," *Quick
Question: New Poems*. Ecco, 2012. 12.

The title "all by myself don't want to be all by myself" is
from "All By Myself," by Eric Carmen, 1975, on *Eric
Carmen*.

"No one belongs here more than you" is from Miranda
July, *No One Belongs Here More Than You: Stories*.
Scribner, 2008.

Both the title "when women were birds" and the poem's
quotation, "words fly out of our mouths like threatened
birds," are from Terry Tempest Williams, "Variation XV,"
When Women Were Birds: Fifty-Four Variations on Voice.
Reprint edition. Picador, 26 February 2013.

In "mean free path" the quote "you were always on my mind" is from "Always on My Mind," 1972, with lyrics by Wayne Carson, Johnny Christopher, and Mark James.

The title "rarely often always never known" is from John Keats, *Otho the Great: A Tragedy in Five Acts*, 1.1.139.

The title "speak low if you speak love" is from William Shakespeare, *Much Ado About Nothing*, 2.1.91.

In "love is a difficult cause to demonstrate" the lines "a man dwells / within one life whereas a woman lives in / several more but seldom one of her own" is a variation of the lines "a man they say is what he does he lives one life alone … a woman leads a dozen lives and seldom one of her own," from "Where is Me," 2005, with lyrics by Bill Charlap, on *Love is Here to Stay*.

In "petite sonatine cantique" the quote "argue argue argue with me endlessly" is from Elizabeth Bishop, "Argument," *Poems: North and South/A Cold Spring*. Houghton Mifflin Company, the Riverside Press, 1955.

The title "rhetorical pawns in unwinnable arguments" is from Maggie Nelson, "Who We Are," *The Art of Cruelty: A Reckoning*. W.W. Norton & Company, 2012.

In "after an argument the dark mind of night" the quote "error is too early regret is too late" is from Adonis, "Singular in a Plural Form," Body, section 5, A Third Piece, *Selected Poems*. Margellos World Republic of Letters series, Yale University Press, 2010. 156.

In "infinite meadow" the quote "words … are crude and they're also too busy" is from Susan Sontag, "The Aesthetics of Silence," *Styles of Radical Will*. Picador, 2002.

In "she knows he thinks he knows who she is" the quote "self-deception remains the most difficult deception" is from Joan Didion, "On Self-Respect," *Slouching Towards Bethlehem: Essays*. Farrar, Straus and Giroux, 2008.

The title "before behind between above below" is from the John Donne poem, "To His Mistress Going to Bed."

The title "all of me why not take all of me" is from "All of Me," 1931, with lyrics by Gerald Marks and Seymour Simons.

The title "in the way that most of the wind happens" is from Paul Muldoon, "Wind and Tree," *Selected Poems 1968-2014*. Farrar, Straus and Giroux, 2017.

The title "neither proving you less wanted nor less dear" is from Elizabeth Bishop, "Argument," *Poems: North and South/A Cold Spring*. Houghton Mifflin Company, the Riverside Press, 1955.

The title and quote "eloquence is heard but poetry is overheard" is from John Stuart Mill, "What is Poetry," section 1, *Thoughts on Poetry and its Varieties*. Kessinger Publishing, 2010.